ENDURINT:

Chris Sandy's Life After Causing Death

&

Eric Krug's Story of Deadly Decisions

Two Different Stories of Drunk Driving: Two Very Different Prisons

www.chrissandy.com

ISBN: 978-0-9895556-0-9

Printed in the United States of America by

Scott Lithographing Co., Inc.

Book cover design and layout by Fatmac Graphics

Chris Sandy with Wife Jennifer, Madison and Zachary

About the Author

Chris Sandy is a motivational speaker, life coach, author, and mentor. He has traveled to over thirty-five states and spoken to more than one million students, parents, educators, and military service members across the United States.

Chris' story was featured in the Double Emmy Award Winning Television Documentary, **Enduring Regret: Chris Sandy's Story of Living Life After Causing Death**. This documentary has been viewed by millions of people across the world.

Chris uses his life journey to connect with teens and young adults about choices and consequences. Chris truly cares about his audience and is considered one of the best messengers in the youth industry. Chris' mission is to motivate people to accomplish goals, overcome adversity, and make choices matter!

Chris Sandy is married to his beautiful wife, Jennifer. They are raising their two children, Madison and Zachary, and their two dogs, Boomer and Sadie, outside of Atlanta, Georgia.

Dedication

I have a lot of people to thank for supporting me, and if I start trying to list everyone I will undoubtedly leave people out. Please know that I dedicate this book to every person who has believed in me or who has been impacted by poor choices, especially drinking and driving.

My dad is someone I miss every day of my life and I know he would be proud of this accomplishment. Dad, this is for you, too.

There is a special group of people who truly helped me along the way, whether it was the original or the revised version of this book. Thank you to my mom, Chad, Jim, Jennifer, Madison, Zachary, Joyce, Jack, and Eric.

Mom, I love you and cannot thank you enough for all you have done for me.

I also want to include my sister, Angela, and her family, especially Christopher.

Finally, thank you to all my family members, whether they're on Mom's side, Dad's side, or on my wife's side. Please know that you mean the world to me.

Chris Sandy's Story

Eric Krug's Story

The Story Behind Chris Sandy and Eric Krug

Setting the Stage

As the time approaches for me to take my place on stage, the thought of reliving the most horrific night of my life again almost causes me to walk away from what I know must be done. Mentally returning to the scene is required. These young people in my audience need to become closely acquainted with the consequences of choosing to drink and drive, or deciding to get into a car with someone who has been drinking. They need to become intensely aware that life is fragile and precious, without having to live through an experience that will painfully teach that lesson.

On the giant screen overhead is a picture of me in prison. I walk purposefully to the computer to forward to the next picture, an image of a prison cell. My story begins.

"I spent 3,117 days in a cell just like this one because of a choice I made. I drank. I drove. I killed two innocent people."

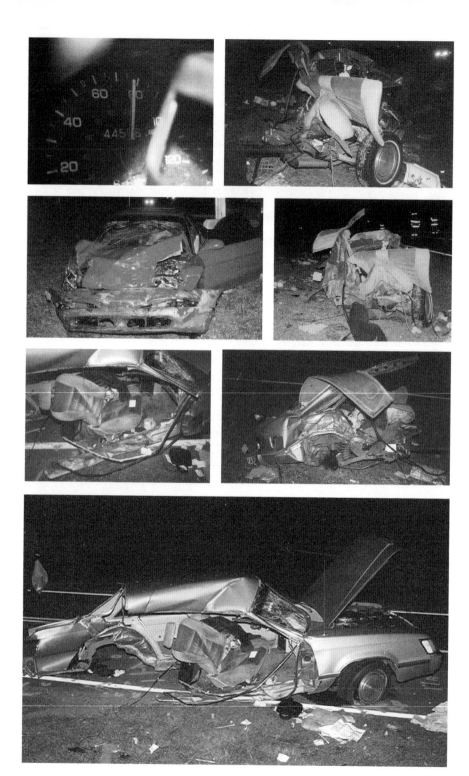

Chris Sandy's Story

Chapter 1

A Horrific Night

"There is a fatality on the scene! There is a fatality on the scene!"

On April 11, 2000, I made a choice I will regret for the rest of my life. I was returning from work that evening and decided to have a little get-together at my house. I picked up some alcohol at the store and proceeded to have more than a few drinks. I slammed four big drinks, back to back. By this time, I had a good buzz and was ready for some excitement. Within a few minutes, I got a call from some friends. They were ready to party, so I decided to drive to their house. My friend, Jesse, climbed into the passenger seat and we drove off. Unfortunately, we never made it to the next party.

Kim and Rebel, my roommates, had offered to drive, but I did not think that was necessary. I felt like my night was just getting started. I was twenty-two years old and four drinks did not seem like a big deal to my friends and me. The radio was blasting, the sunroof was open, and Jesse and I were more than ready to get to the next party.

I was driving down a country road just outside of Atlanta, Georgia. This two-lane road was a short cut to my friend's house. I knew it very well. I started flying down this little road, braked for the stop sign, and made a quick left turn. The speed limit was 35 mph, but within a few seconds, I was pushing 80 mph and was not about to slow down. Many of us had sped down this road before, so no big deal. We were just having fun and enjoying life on the edge. I thought I knew my limits.

As we came around a sharp curve, there was a white minivan ahead in my lane. The only thought in my head was getting to this party to hook up with my friends. So, without hesitation, I decided to blow past the minivan. I was driving in the right lane, doing 80 mph, when I drifted over into the left lane to pass the minivan. Suddenly, there was a car in front of me heading in my direction. The car in the oncoming lane had its left turn signal on. As I tried to get back into my lane, a brilliant flash shot in front of my eyes and my ears flooded with an incredibly loud BANG! The sound was intensely horrifying, haltingly sudden, and was felt in every bone in my body. Then, everything went black.

As the next few seconds passed, I could not see anything. Once the car came to a stop, my eyes flew open. I was pinned between the front windshield and the dashboard and could hardly breathe. I couldn't see Jesse, nor could I focus on the idea of what had just happened. Upon finding the door and crawling out onto the pavement, I noticed something was wrong with my leg. My right leg had been dislocated from my hip and had rolled over onto my back. My right knee was bleeding severely. It had been thrust into the dashboard next to the steering wheel, ripping the skin off the inside part of my knee. I was in tremendous pain and was barely able to move. The pain came in pulses seemingly tied into every heartbeat, and it only got worse with each passing second.

Shortly after I exited the car, a gentleman ran over to check on me. I asked, "What happened to my friend? Is he ok?"

The man did not really answer me and instead just said, "Lie still and calm down. Help is on the way."

As I lay there, I thought I must have turned my wheel and wrecked on the side of the road. I just could not imagine smashing into that other car, but it happened so fast, I really had no idea. The pain was so intense that I went into shock just before losing consciousness.

The next time I briefly regained consciousness, there was an officer standing over me. The officer informed me he needed to ask me some questions before I was airlifted from the scene. He asked, "Do you know how fast you were going?"

I replied, "No sir."

That was obviously a lie. I knew I was speeding, but I

did not want to get into any more trouble.

Next, the officer asked, "Is there someone we can contact for you?"

I think I gave him my mom's name and number. The officer wanted to contact a family member because this was a horrific crash, and he wanted to inform my family of the situation and tell them which hospital I was being sent to.

The officer leaned closer in order to detect an odor and asked, "Have you been drinking?"

I immediately said, "No."

I did not want to go to jail for drinking and driving. I was already thinking the situation was bad enough, and I was attempting to avoid the possibility of going to jail for a DUI/DWI.

As I was lying there on the side of the road, worrying about going to jail, I heard someone yell in the background. I have no idea who was yelling. It could have been a paramedic, firefighter, or deputy sheriff.

"There is a fatality on the scene! There is a fatality on the scene!"

At that very moment, I realized I had just killed someone. Someone was dead because of something I had done. I started praying that this was just a horrible nightmare. I was hoping that when my eyes closed, everything would go away.

Chapter 2
The Hospital

After opening my eyes and glancing around the surroundings, I knew I was in a hospital. Before I could formulate another thought, the stark realization swept in like a raging storm: I had killed somebody, ruined my own life, and who knew what else? Those thoughts were constantly running through my head. I got sick at that very moment and threw up on myself. The smell of regurgitated alcohol was gross. I could barely move, so a nurse had to come and wipe up the vomit. I now knew for sure this was not a bad dream. It was a living nightmare, and it was only just beginning.

Once I was cleaned up, several friends and family came in to visit. The person I recall the most during those first few visits was my friend Keri.

She came walking into my room and sat right next to me and said, "Chris, do you remember anything about last night? Do you have any idea what actually happened?"

I slowly turned toward her, looked into her eyes and said, "I heard them yell it on the side of the road. I know I just killed someone. Please don't tell me anything else."

Keri could not look me in the eyes, but glanced away and whispered, "Chris, there were two people in that other car. They are both dead."

I was stunned. I knew there was one person, but knowing there were two people who had died was overwhelming. I looked straight up at the ceiling, and thought to myself, I can't believe I killed two innocent people. They are dead. What was I thinking? How could I have been so dumb and irresponsible?

Later on I told my mom I had no idea there were two people killed in the crash, but she informed me that I talked to her in the emergency room and told her two people were killed. To this day I still cannot remember talking to my mom. I honestly do not remember finding out about the two people dying in the crash until Keri told me the horrible news.

I was expecting the police to come in and arrest me any minute. I did not know much about the law, so I really had no idea what I would face for being responsible for such a horrific crash. Knowing I had ended the lives of two people and ruined the lives of so many others, all as a result of a stupid choice, was more than I could grasp.

There could have easily been more lives lost. As I lay there, I thought about Jesse, the passenger in my car, who was one of the funniest people you could meet. I remembered how we were cutting up and laughing as I sped down the country road with the radio blasting. I remembered seeing Jesse out of the corner of my eye reaching across to grab his seat belt just as I started passing the minivan. Neither of us had been wearing one. That seat belt saved his life. Jesse was conscious after the crash, so he had to witness the chaos and horrifying events.

Jesse and I have spoken a few times since my release from prison, but all we can talk about are the events from the crash. We share a few haunting memories from that night. He wishes we would have been smarter as young people. I obviously made a horrible choice to drive drunk and let Jesse get into my car. When Jesse was in my car, he was my responsibility. I almost killed my friend. If he had not strapped on his seat belt, he would have been dead, too. Thankfully, Jesse is not mad at me, but he has been left with a painful memory that he will have to endure for the rest of his life. His life will never be the same, and that night will never escape his thoughts.

During my stay at the hospital, I had minimal care because I only had liability insurance. The hospital should not have even treated me. Trying to imagine what the victims' family was going through made me question why I had been allowed to live. Back then, I truly wished I would have died.

After five days, I was released from the hospital. I just knew the police were going to arrest me and take me to jail. I could barely stand up, even with the use of crutches. I was in a lot of pain, and was terrified of going to jail in that shape. To be quite honest, I was scared to death of going to jail, period. My family escorted me out of the hospital, and my dad drove me to my parents' house. The rest of the day was a total blur. I was consumed with the untold consequences of my bad choices. I knew I was going to be arrested at any moment, convicted without hesitation, and locked away forever.

STATEMENT - TRAFFIC

Name ___Shanna R. ▓▓▓▓▓▓▓▓___   Address ▓▓▓▓▓▓▓▓▓▓▓▓▓▓▓

Telephone No. ▓▓▓▓▓▓▓▓ Age __34__ Occupation ▓▓▓▓▓▓▓▓▓▓▓▓▓▓▓▓▓
▓▓▓▓▓▓▓▓▓▓▓▓▓▓

Location Where
Statement Made ___Jack Neely Rd.___ Hour __9:15 pm__ Date __4/11/00__

Location of Undersigned
At Time of Event ___at accident scene___

STATEMENT MADE BY ABOVE NAMED PERSON

I was traveling down Jack Neely Rd towards Kirkland, at the curve, the Red Car (Prore?) passed me on a curve, double yellow line going very very fast. I slowed down, up ahead I saw a car coming down Jack Neely away from Kirkland, and the car had its left turn signal on. The car that passed me (the Red One) was not in the Proper lane at the time he passed me, he was traveling in the middle of the road. Then I saw the Red Car hit the Tan/Brown Car and the Red Car went into the ditch, the tan/Brown car spun around and stopped. I called 911, pulled over, to check the people. One man in car (Brown) did not respond. One lady in grass, no response. I did not check the Red Car.
Please call if I can help any
Thank you.

(USE REVERSE SIDE IF NECESSARY)
WITNESSED BY: ___Shanna ▓▓▓▓▓▓▓▓▓▓___ STATEMENT MADE BY: _____

DPS-1000(10/77)

Chapter 3
Arrested and Charged

As days passed, thoughts of my probable arrest loomed. I was taking prescription pain medication for my leg and trying to numb the guilt of my actions. Corporal Scott Short from the Georgia State Patrol showed up at my parents' house to interview me. He was part of the Specialized Collision Reconstruction Team (SCRT), which specialized in motor vehicle crashes with fatalities. I simply told Corporal Short what happened. He stopped the interview on several occasions, as I had to gather myself; my emotions were uncontrollable at times, talking about the crash. The memory was haunting and painful. As I described my actions, I was sickened by the reality of what I had done. During the interview, I altered the truth because I was scared to death of the consequences. Corporal Short was not new to this type of interview, and he knew the evidence spoke for itself. He did not need the interview for the conviction.

A few months later, I was charged with two counts of vehicular homicide by DUI and reckless driving. A deputy sheriff was sent to my parents' house to serve a warrant for my arrest. When my mom told me that a warrant had been issued for my arrest, I turned myself into the police. I was arrested and booked.

One of the big factors in my arrest was that my blood alcohol content (BAC) at the time of the crash was 0.14.

In 2000, the legal limit for anyone twenty-one years old or older in the state of Georgia was .10, so I was clearly over that limit. With a blood alcohol content of .08, most people are buzzed and their reactions are slowed. This combination makes the roads hazardous even for those who are abiding by the rules.

Unfortunately, I did not respect the law nor listen to authorities and educators, and look what happened. Becoming complacent when drinking and choosing to drive is negligent and reckless. As I have learned, such behavior is extremely selfish. Even the choice to ride with someone who has been drinking is ignorant and selfish. Taking that risk can result in painful consequences, not just for you, but for your friends and family.

My family was worried to death about me while I was locked up. After a couple of weeks in jail, I was released. My bail was $20,000. My parents were able to post my bond, which was $2,000. Posting bond typically means paying a bondsman around 10% of the actual bail to get released out of jail. Since a bondsman posted my bail, if I did not show up to court, my parents would be responsible for the full $20,000. A bondsman will also accept deeds to property, but if you miss court, they gain full possession of the property (house, car, etc.). A lot of people cannot post bond because they do not have enough credit or they cannot cover the cost.

I was glad to get out of that dungeon. I was scared and terrified of going back to jail. Little did I know, I would be spending a lot more time in that environment than I could have ever imagined.

GEORGIA STATE PATROL
INCIDENT REPORT

Date	Name of Trooper Completing Report	Post
04-11-00	TROOPER ~~XXXXXX XXXXXXX~~	48

COURT SYSTEM	NEWTON COUNTY		

INCIDENT		LOCATION OF OCCURANCE
D.U.I.		JACK NEELY

NAME AND ADDRESS OF PERSONS ARRESTED	RACE	SEX	DATE OF BIRTH
CHRISTOPHER JOHN SANDY ~~XXXXXXXXXXX~~ S.E. CONYERS, GA 30013	W	M	06-21-77

WITNESSES NAME AND ADDRESS	RACE	SEX	DATE OF BIRTH

REMARKS CONCERNING INCIDENT

ON APRIL 11, 2000 AT APPROXIMATELY 10:46 P.M., I WAS AT ATLANTA MEDICAL CENTER TO HAVE BLOOD DRAWN FROM CHRISTOPHER SANDY. AFTER THE BLOOD WAS DRAWN, I CONTINUED ON MY REGULAR PATROL AND KEPT THE SEALED BLOOD KIT IN THE FRONT SEAT OF MY PATROL CAR. AT 6:00 A.M., I TURNED THE SEALED BLOOD KIT OVER TO C.E.O. MICHAEL BROWN AT THE STATE PATROL POST IN CONYERS.

Code Section Violated	Quantity of drugs on or in reach of person	Type test conducted if drug related	RESULTS	LOCATION OF TEST
		BLOOD		
		BREATH		
		URINE		
		OTHER		

OTHER RELATED REPORTS		OTHER OFFICERS WHO ASSISTED WITH ARREST
Citation Number	Accident Report Number	

~~XXXXXXXXXXXXXX~~
Signature of Officer

5-25-00
Date

DPS 1113

27

Chapter 4
Out on Bond

The trip from the jail to my parents' home was a long and quiet drive. Mom and I were at a loss as to what to say to each other. Life had been, and was being, marred in an irreparable way.

My sister, Angela, and I had the best parents any two children could have ever imagined. They adopted us from birth because they could not have children. Mom and Dad provided us with opportunities, a good education, and taught us right from wrong. They would do anything for us, but I let them down in so many ways. In hindsight, I now know how much I disappointed my dad when I quit playing football, soccer, and basketball. Both of my parents supported my decision and wanted me to make choices that were in my interest, not theirs. They trusted me and thought I would make the right choices because of the way they had raised me. I should have never quit sports. I loved playing defensive tackle and being the place kicker and punter. I just did not want to work as hard anymore and I wanted to hang out with friends and go to parties on weekends. My parents had no idea how that one decision was going to drastically affect all our lives. In my way of thinking, I ruined their dreams of a great family. They would disagree, but I know I could have made better choices.

A part of my mom thought it would have been better if I had died in the crash. I know that sounds horrible, and my mom probably does not like the idea of me mentioning her belief at the time, but it is the truth. She was terrified of the suffering I would have to go through and the painful consequences I would undoubtedly face. Shortly thereafter, she steadily relied on her faith and was ready to stand by me through the terrible ordeal. My mom was ready to sacrifice everything to help me through this nightmare. I love my mom and all she has done for me. I did not deserve it, but she loved and still loves me unconditionally. A child cannot ask any more than that from a parent.

Shortly after being released on bond, Dad, Mom, and I went to visit a public defender. Public defenders are appointed by the courts. We were in that office for maybe five minutes when the attorney looked at us and said, "I believe you should just plead guilty and hopefully receive a fifteen-year sentence. That is the best deal you will get."

We got up, walked out, and from that moment on we knew I was going to prison. It was now just a matter of how long my sentence would be: fifteen, twenty, or thirty years.

There was no arguing the fact of my guilt. Confronting that fact was difficult for my parents. Spending the next fifteen or thirty years in prison was not how my parents envisioned my life. My family was also trying to get acclimated to the judicial process. Court proceedings can be challenging and arduous to understand. We were unfamiliar with the process, and the public defender was unwilling to give us any options, so my family decided to hire an attorney. We needed legal advice about how to handle this situation.

There is a business side to legal proceedings. When my attorney instructed me to initially plead "not guilty", that was only to buy some more time to figure out what we were going to do next. The legalities of the courtroom were very confusing because I had absolutely no intention to imply that I was without guilt, but I had to go through the legal process. There were several court appearances to allow specific motions to be filed. As painful the proceedings were for my family and me, they were even more painful for the family of the victims.

Being out on bond was difficult. My friends tried to help by distracting me from the fact that I had killed two people and was soon going to prison for a long time. I was drinking and using drugs to numb the pain. I wanted to die. I did not want to live after what I had done. I drank and did whatever I could to kill my own fear and guilt. I would rather have been numbered among the victims. Who would want to continue living with this kind of guilt? Though I understood my problems, I had not yet learned how to cope with my guilt without the use of drugs and alcohol.

In the midst of all this chaos, I was dating Laurie. She was in college, studying to be a teacher. She honestly kept me afloat. If she had not been so supportive, I would have drowned in my sorrow and guilt. Laurie was an awesome person, caring for me in the worst of times. She was a great friend, and a person I will forever respect. It is hard to find people who are genuine friends. We pick friends thinking they are going to be true to us no matter the circumstances. Those intentions are based on a blue sky reality, but genuine friendship is not determined by how well we celebrate the good times, but instead by how effectively we navigate the thunderstorms that invade all relationships. The rule is golden for that reason. Treat others as you would want to be treated. Friends are supposed to help lift each other up and push each other to be successful. Friends are there to support and guide each other through the good times and the bad. Really look at the friends you have now and ask yourself, "Are they good for me?"

I realize those friends truly wanted to help and were impacted by my choice to drive after drinking, but I regret we did not understand the meaning of friendship. We should not have accepted the social norms of our generation and should have been more concerned about the well-being of each person's future. Nevertheless, I wish them all well!

While on bond, I tried staying busy. I was working in heating and air-conditioning, installing equipment. My boss, Calvin, knew what I did, but continued to allow me to work on his crew. As a matter of fact, he picked me up every day because I did not drive after the crash. Each day was a struggle.

It is amazing that I did not commit suicide during this time. You can be sure it was considered. I'm glad I didn't do it because that would have only caused more pain in the lives of the people I love. There were many times I wanted my life to end, or wanted to escape to a foreign country, like Mexico. Running off and hiding in another country like some movie script is not real life. People that run get caught and face even deeper consequences. I remember my dad giving me the best advice.

He said, "It is what it is. You really messed up, but if you will face this situation like a man and take responsibility for your actions, I will stand by your side every step of the way."

From that day forward, my dad taught me to be a man and take responsibility for my actions. That is something every person should learn to do rather than blaming others for their problems. Be accountable for what you say and do.

Chapter 5
Judgment Day
Here on Earth

The phone rang and it was my attorney. A court date had been set and a plea agreement to serve ten years in prison was being discussed. I was emotionally and physically exhausted, but knew it was time. We appeared in court, and the victims' family and prosecutor rejected the plea for ten years to serve. My heart sank. I could not fathom serving ten years in prison, and now they were saying that ten years was not punishment enough. A few days later, an agreement was reached by all parties involved for me to receive a sentence of thirteen years in prison followed by seventeen years on probation. One horrible choice to drink and drive resulted in two lost lives and a thirty-year sentence. The pain, caused by my actions, was irreversible.

On April 10, 2001, we all piled into the car and drove to the courthouse. My emotions were like a bundle of raw nerves and sleep had eluded me the night before. As our car began moving, I felt as though we were in a hearse heading for the cemetery. When we pulled into the courthouse parking lot, many of my friends were already standing there waiting for me. As soon as I stepped out of the car and started walking toward the courthouse, the idea to run and never look back flashed through my head.

I was shaking as we entered the courthouse. My lawyer, Bruce Morriss, greeted us in the hallway and informed me that the victims' family was seated on the right side of the courtroom. We all walked in together and sat up front. Bruce showed the plea agreement to me, but I barely comprehended what was truly taking place. By signing that document, I was agreeing that my irresponsible choices and reprehensible behavior would prevent me from living in society for a period of thirteen years and that I would be supervised by the state of Georgia for seventeen years following my incarceration.

Judge Ott addressed everyone in the courtroom, and then looked at me while handing down the sentence. Tears started rolling down both sides of my face and my stomach was in knots. Once the sentence was read, the judge gave me an opportunity to address the courtroom, specifically the victims' family. I walked to the front of the courtroom, turned around, and then completely broke down. Judge Ott turned and told me to remove myself from the stand until I was in control of my emotions. I stepped aside, pulled myself together, and looked out at my family, friends, and most importantly, the victims' family.

Then I began to speak. "I am very sorry for the pain

I caused, and I know that there is nothing I can do to fix what I have done. I am sorry, extremely sorry, for my actions. I promise to someday make something positive happen from this horrifying experience. I do not know how that will be possible, but I will try."

My tears were streaming uncontrollably. A sheriff deputy placed a set of handcuffs on me and escorted me out of the courtroom. Tuesday, April 10, 2001 marked my last moment of complete freedom for the next thirty years.

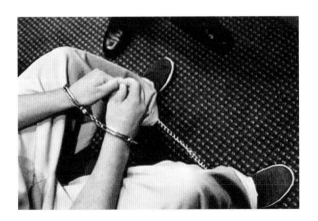

Chapter 6
Jail to Prison

The county jail was my temporary place of residence while I waited to go to real prison. I was placed in a high-security cellblock, an atmosphere that had me on guard at all times. My bunkmate, Chi-Town, was a gang member from Chicago. We managed to get along fairly well, although I learned quickly that trust was an exceedingly rare commodity behind bars. You had to constantly be on alert while always looking over your shoulder. During the first couple of days, I had to quickly adjust to the way of life in the county jail. Unwritten rules governing bathrooms, showers, and dealing with other convicts and officers were essential, but not clear. Basically, life behind bars is a subculture of its own. I remember learning how to light a cigarette with a broken razor blade, AA batteries, and a metal stool. Back then, I thought smoking was pretty cool, but smoking was nothing but a hassle and waste of money. Thank goodness I quit that habit a couple of years into my sentence. I also witnessed people making shanks, which are homemade knives or pointed objects with a handle used for stabbing other prisoners or staff. The atmosphere reeked with an odor that was reflective of poor choices.

There is an established pecking order in the slammer. As a prisoner, you are a part of the pecking order voluntarily or unwillingly; it does not matter. There was a convict named Philpot. He was a 350-pound black guy who could be considered slightly tilted. Philpot also had a lazy eye, which had a tendency to make him look even crazier. I never had any issues with Philpot, but he always joked about how he would like to go a few rounds with me. Remember what I said about the pecking order. When entering that environment, I weighed 260 pounds, so I was not a lightweight. He felt as though I would give him a good fight and earn him some points. Those with ringside seats wondered whether I had earned any points from being jokingly challenged by Philpot or lost points because I had not accepted. Several days later, four guys tried jumping Philpot and stabbing him with pencils and razors. Those four stooges regretted that attempt at challenging the established pecking order. After that, they did whatever Philpot asked: cleaned his cell, did his laundry, gave him food, money, and anything else he wanted to stop him from inflicting any more pain.

The county jail had not been renovated prior to me arriving. In fact, it was very old, dirty, and dark. With almost no imagination, the place could be mistaken for a dungeon. We just sat in that dark, murky place playing cards – mostly Spades. I was a good card player and those Spade games would sometimes get a little out of control because of all the trash talking and gambling. I also spent time reading books (from a very limited selection), writing letters, and trying to avoid all the fighting.

Family and friends would always be there for visitation, but visits were always bittersweet. We were separated by concrete and glass, and our conversations were through a phone. There was always the concern that staff members were listening to our phone conversations. Privacy was nonexistent.

Going outside was a rarity. Most of our time was spent in a dreary cellblock in our orange jumpsuits. A night never passed without me thinking about the crash. The haunting thought that I was going to be in prison for more than 4,700 days and nights was almost unimaginable. Stories were always circulating about prisoners trying to protect themselves and in the process killing another inmate or being killed. Prison is not a reprieve from the streets. It is a demeaning, debilitating, and loathsome place loaded with unthinkable stories that are far more fact than fiction. In the county jail, I actually felt like I still had friends. People wrote, visited, and accepted my collect phone calls from the pay phone within the cellblock. The calls were really expensive. Phone bills could reach hundreds of dollars in a matter of weeks.

On June 1, 2001, I was transferred to Jackson Diagnostic State Prison. Early that morning, I heard the guards yell, "Pack it up, Sandy." That meant it was my time to go down the road to prison. I was shaking the minute I realized what was happening. I had heard all kinds of scary things about Jackson.

I remembered driving by it several years before all this happened and thinking to myself, man, I would kill myself before ending up in a place like that.

Ironically, I was now heading to Georgia's maximum-security prison, where death row prisoners are housed awaiting execution. We were all loaded onto a van wearing shackles, handcuffs, and leg irons (see picture). We were chained together. I remember feeling so dirty from the county jail and relieved to get out of there, but relief was replaced with fear about what might lie ahead. I would soon learn that the county jail was nothing compared to a state penitentiary.

After traveling for less than an hour, I could feel the cuffs cutting into my wrists and ankles. Everyone in the van was coping with their anxious energy by talking about anything to whomever would listen. As we approached Jackson on that long winding road, all nervous chatter immediately turned to silence.

Jackson is a maximum-security prison housing over two thousand inmates who have committed every kind of crime imaginable. When we pulled up to this intimidating facility, there was so much razor wire we could barely see through the security fences. I noticed guard towers placed at strategic points all around the prison. The gates opened, the correctional officers did a search of the van, and the van was finally permitted to enter the compound.

Once the van stopped, about twenty correctional officers stormed toward us. We unloaded, stepped onto the pavement, and immediately realized the nightmare was beginning. The officers made a strong point to make sure we understood that individual freedom was a thing of the past.

Intake was where the nightmare began. It was not a large room. I just remember seeing four yellow lines, some showers, and a few chairs. I would soon become familiar with the entire room. Once we stepped into the processing room, they told all fifty of us to stand on the yellow lines and strip buck naked. After we stripped, we were instructed to get into the showers, and the correctional officers sprayed us down with something that deloused us from the nasty jail environments from where we had come. We sat in the chairs and our heads were shaved. I believe it was a process to break us down, and believe me, it worked. Even if you don't have to go through this kind of process, by the time you are actually in prison you feel dehumanized. We had to go through all kinds of testing throughout the day. Testing for physical health and mental health. This was part of the classification process. At the end of the day, we were all sent to a cellblock or open dormitory.

I was escorted to F-House, a building considered a cell house, which was on lockdown for twenty-three hours every day. Lock yourself in your closet for twenty-three hours and you will get a small sampling of the feeling I had. Setting foot in this place was eerie. It made the hair on the back of my neck stand up. This was an old prison with bars. One like you would see in the movies, especially old ones, like Shawshank Redemption or Alcatraz. There was a top tier and a bottom tier and no air-conditioning. It felt like 120 degrees inside and there were just a few large fans blowing hot air around. The place was big, intimidating, and very uncomfortable.

An officer looked at me and grunted, "Hey, go to the top and get in cell 225." I grabbed my small bag of state-provided belongings and started walking. Once I arrived at 225, I stopped. The correctional officer hit a button, and the cell door barely slid open. I pulled the door back, stepped inside the tiny cell, and the officer yelled, "Shut the door!"

Of course I was scared to death, so I immediately shut the door. There were hundreds of people locked in this cellblock and it was so loud in there, I felt like I was going crazy. My brain was barely functioning and my thoughts were totally scattered. The cells were all concrete and steel, so it took a while to adjust to the echoing of voices and all the loud sounds coming from other convicts beating on lockers and beds. I had to pull myself together. In an environment like this, people can smell fear on you.

In the beginning, it was sheer madness. An older guy sitting on the bottom bunk, my new cellmate for twenty-three hours a day, said, "What's up dude? Welcome to this miserable place."

I had no idea who this guy was or what he was in prison for, but I was so overwhelmed with the atmosphere, I didn't even care. I just looked at him and said, "This is crazy and messed up. Does it get any better?"

The guy smirked and said, "Son, it ain't gonna get any better."

I was ready for anything to happen. Living in the free world beyond the walls of confinement and razor wire surrounding the compound was a thing of the past.

My mind was reeling from being in prison. I jumped up to the top bunk to lie down. This was the end of the day, so shortly after my head hit the raw, cotton-filled pillow, the call for lights out was made. For whatever reason, that cellblock fell silent. You could have heard a roll-up (hand rolled cigarette) hit the floor. As I lay on that thin cotton bed, with my body pushing through to the steel bed frame, all I could think about was how this could be my future home for the next 4,745 days. I decided I'd rather be dead. Sharing a tiny cell for twenty-three hours a day was difficult to say the least. Sitting on a toilet while someone was in the bed only inches away from you was not pleasant. My cellmate and I talked, but we were hardly friends. We were just acquaintances trying to make it through each day. You either learn to get along or you end up fighting. Those fights result in being hauled off by correctional officers to solitary confinement, or even worse, getting killed. Some inmates cannot tolerate each other and will start fighting ferociously. It can get really ugly when you're locked in a cell for twenty-three hours a day.

Honestly, being locked in a cell for any period of time can get extremely dangerous if you do not get along with your cellmate. I will never forget when two guys on the bottom range (main floor) started fighting. We could hear every punch and kick that landed until blood started flowing out of the cell. Everyone could see the blood and everyone knew it was bad. I do not know what happened to the guy who suffered all the blows, but when he was hauled off on a stretcher not moving, I could only imagine.

Sharing experiences like this could be an entire book by itself. I am only sharing a few moments of life in my beginning stages of prison, but trying to describe the feelings of everyday life in the penitentiary for eight and a half years is almost impossible. The one thing I knew for sure was that survival in prison was not guaranteed.

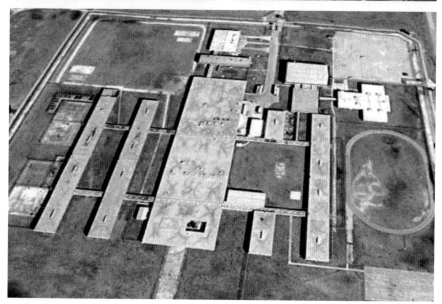

Chapter 7
Life in Prison

I was housed at Jackson for four long months. You might not think that is a long time, but believe me, it is longer than you can imagine. Being on lockdown for twenty-three hours every day makes each minute sixty countable seconds long. The toilets were out in the open with no doors and no stalls. We were allowed to shower three times a week: Tuesday, Thursday, and Saturday. We showered about fifty at a time, and yes, we would joke when someone "dropped the soap". Although everyone was joking, most prisoners did not even attempt to pick up the soap, even if it left them without. When rape occurs in prison, it does not happen when people drop the soap. Some of the worst people on this earth are locked up in prison, and they do not need an excuse to carry out their heinous deeds. You never know what will happen on any given day when you wake up in a penitentiary, whether it is a maximum-, medium-, or minimum-security prison. A prison by any name is still a prison.

Learning to survive in prison was a day-by-day experience. Everyone was always trying to trade something to get something. For example, there is a commissary, which is a store for inmates where you can purchase food and personal hygiene items. We were able to order from the commissary once a week. The selections were slim, and we had a spending limit, but store items helped you get by without having to always eat the prison food. The main items were Ramen noodle soups, coffee, chips, cigarettes, Little Debbies, and hygiene products. These items are currency in prison. On the other hand, if an inmate caused any trouble or did not follow instructions given by a correctional officer or staff, he would go to the hole (isolation) or be written up (served with a disciplinary report). Such infractions were costly: five dollars for each write-up, loss of store, rec-yard, or library privileges, or having to spend extended periods of time in isolation.

At Jackson, they did not allow smoking, but people would still get their hands on tobacco. A pack of Bugler, which is a pouch of loose tobacco with some rolling papers, could go for between sixty and one hundred dollars. Cigarettes could easily get you sent to the hole, beat up, or even stabbed. Prison is a subculture of the worst kind.

Thinking back on all that mess, I remember my first confrontation. Everybody was on lockdown, but one of the many unwritten rules was that each person was responsible for passing items from one cell to the next. Mostly cigarettes or wicks (lit twists of paper used for lighting cigarettes) were passed around. One guy on the block, who was probably never getting out of prison, would knock out his cell light and strike the electrical wires together to ignite a wick. That was called "the shine". Once someone yelled for shine, they normally had to pay the shine man for a cigarette and the wick would be passed down. That meant each person had to participate. One day, I was sick of jumping up and down out of my bunk to pass the shine. I was stressed out and frustrated because I just wanted to lie in my bunk and not move for a while.

I finally said, "I am not getting down again to pass the shine. Make your own wick!"

As soon as the doors popped open to go to chow (mealtime), my neighbor and I started fighting right there. It was crazy. We stopped before the correctional officers made it up to us so we did not have to go to the hole. That was my first big taste of life in prison.

When the doors popped open, I had to be prepared for whatever might happen, even when I had no idea that something was brewing. I made the mistake of getting involved in the cigarette black market at the beginning of my time. I realized how stupid it was and how that kind of behavior was contrary to my newly acquired commitment toward change in my life. Why add more trouble to my life? I needed to learn how to live my life in a manner now that would reflect how I wanted to live my life once I got out of prison.

Jackson was, and still is, an extremely volatile place, and a major sigh of relief came over my entire being when I was told again to pack it up. I was transferred out of Jackson on September 11, 2001, a day our whole country will never forget. We had a visitation scheduled for that day, and my mom had driven down to visit with me at Jackson, but I was gone. She was terrified and wanted to know which prison I had been transferred to, but for security reasons they were not allowed to tell her. She felt helpless because my whereabouts were unknown. Fortunately, the guard at Jackson told her that the next time she saw me, she would be able to hug me.

That morning, all prisoners scheduled to transfer were ordered out of their bunks at 3:30 am by the correctional officers. There is a process of separating your stuff from that which belongs to the state that you have to go through. As I left, lots of thoughts and questions ran through my mind.

Jackson was huge and the state always transferred inmates on Tuesdays and Thursdays, but for some reason we were being transferred on a Friday. They had a bunch of big Blue Bird buses in the parking lot, and we were all lined up with our handcuffs and shackles on. We were loaded onto our designated buses and were taken across the state of Georgia to a number of prisons. Riding on the bus was very strange. How could this really be happening? A haunting question crossed my mind in a haze. I wondered when, if ever, my life would return to any degree of normalcy. While traveling on that bus and viewing the outside world through the steel grate covering the window, I regretted many of the choices I had made in my life. The mounting consequences were all too obvious.

In less than a three-hour bus ride, we arrived at Wheeler Correctional Facility in Wheeler County. It is a medium-security prison located in South Georgia. We slowly stepped off the bus in our leg shackles, entered the prison, and were escorted down a hallway to the intake room. As we sat in a tiny room crunched together, the guy next to me was listening to his AM/FM radio.

He turned to me and everyone else in the holding cell and said, "A couple of planes just hit the World Trade Center. New York is under attack!"

Of course, none of us truly believed him. People in prison lie all the time just to get things stirred up, but the guy turned to me and said, "I'm serious. You can listen for yourself."

I put the headphone close to my right ear, and sure enough, this guy was telling the truth. Everyone in that cell was silent. We were just as stunned as everyone else in the world. People were even starting rumors that if the United States was under attack, one of the first things they would be required to do is eliminate the prison population. On the surface we doubted such tales, but we also knew how society as a whole felt about criminals.

My first day in the new penitentiary was obviously abnormal, but the reality of being in prison was certainly in my face. I was sent to an open dorm. If memory serves me correctly, the dorm number was 100L. Walking in a dorm for the first time is like being a stranger in a strange land while on view. Everybody was scoping me out, sizing me up, and speculating about how I would affect the dorm. I walked back to the bunk to which I was assigned and met my new bunkmate.

I was at Wheeler for only a couple of years, which is a small amount of time in prison-speak. Some choices that were made there could have ruined my chances of achieving some of my very specific goals. I wanted to get out of prison and do something positive. I was just struggling to see the light at the end of the tunnel. I did not know how I could survive for thirteen years in this environment. One day, I realized that if I did not choose to make positive choices while in prison, I would never make them on the outside. I needed to redefine myself, and that needed to begin while in prison.

As if prison is not bad enough, it is worth mentioning how bad the gangs have become in the prisons. They have special gang unit officers in prisons to keep up with everyone. I am glad I never joined a gang in prison. Those kinds of choices always end badly. Strategizing and scheming goes on behind the scenes in prison, almost all with bad intent. Some inmates even use the prison chapel as a place to make illegal transactions with drugs, weapons, and contraband. Even with that element, I am thankful that church services are allowed in prison. That is what started me in the direction of becoming a better person and taught me a lot about how I was to become the man that God intended me to be. I was exposed to many different denominations, and that helped ground me in my beliefs. Spiritual services are critical for inmates in prisons. They are a much needed light in a dark place.

It's important to understand that, even though prison is a negative environment, there are still avenues to educate and better oneself. If a person blames the situation or environment for failure, that individual is just making excuses that can deter opportunities to succeed. Now, do not get me wrong, I am not saying you can mess up, go to prison, and succeed. Honestly, most people who go to prison end up failing in their attempts to better themselves. In prison, people lose hope and become corrupted. When paroled, they are simply felons, and society as a whole is not as willing to offer them a second chance.

While serving time, I had an awesome mentor who helped me stay positive and encouraged me to learn from this terrible mistake. My incredible mentor was Chad Foster. I met Chad about six months before I was sent to prison. He did not judge me. He truly wanted to help. Chad is a motivational speaker, author, and professional fisherman. His story is very interesting, and I would encourage everyone to go to his website www.chadfoster.com to read more about him. He has written many great books, but I highly recommend *Teenagers Preparing for the Real World*. Chad also had his own fly fishing show on ESPN. Did I mention how much I love fishing? Well, I do, and Chad found that out and took me fishing. That day on the little bass boat changed my life. He gave me hope when I was hopeless.

Chad reminded me that most everything was possible if I worked hard toward meeting specific goals. One big goal was to find a way to show others how painful the consequences can be from drinking and driving. I am thankful that he showed me how important it is to help others learn from my poor choice. This has become my mission in life. Chad also taught me the importance of having someone hold you accountable in life. When someone holds you accountable, you work harder and keep yourself more focused on tasks or goals. There were several times in prison when I avoided fights because of Chad. I knew he was my mentor and would hold me accountable, which would be worse than spending a week in the hole in solitary confinement. It is important to find someone who will keep you on track, but you must respect and listen to him or her. My wife holds me accountable now, but that is a whole different story.

Speaking from experience, if I was able to find ways in prison to resolutely hold on to hope and untiringly pursue ways to better myself, then others can most definitely do the same out in the free world. We live in a world with almost unlimited resources, but we have to actively search for them. Wanting to change should be replaced with feeling a need to change. Every person can strive for change, because every person can make himself or herself better.

After spending several years at Wheeler and realizing the importance of making good choices, I had an opportunity to participate in a pilot program for the

Department of Corrections. This was called the Inmate Speaking Program, which would allow certain inmates to tell their stories in hopes of preventing young people from making poor decisions. In order to participate in the program, you had to be selected and approved and agree that this type of program would not get you released from prison earlier than your tentative parole or max-out date. Entering this program was strictly voluntarily. I personally wrote many letters to important people in the Department of Corrections, including the Commissioner, and to the Georgia Governor's Office of Highway Safety, senators, judges, and educators all over the state of Georgia. Being in this program was important to me, and eventually I was selected to be the first inmate for the program.

Shortly after I was selected, I was transferred to another prison called Burruss Correctional Training Center, a medium- and minimum-security prison located in middle Georgia. Just a reminder: prison is prison, no matter how it might be disguised. When you are transferred to a new prison there is always a time of trepidation. As twisted as this may sound, once you are familiar with one nightmare, there is hesitation about being moved to another nightmare, even if it is rumored to be less demented.

Thankfully, the rumors proved to be true. I had experienced worse, but that did not mean the facility was safe. No penitentiary is safe. Anything can happen at any given moment in prison. While at Burruss, I witnessed more than my share of fights, and was involved in a few, a fact of which I am not proud. Activities were the same as the other nightmares, but to a lesser degree. There were stabbings, but not as severe. Inmates were raped, but not as savagely. Prisoners were attacked, but not as brutally.

I remember one of my cellmates named Gary, who had been in prison for forty-two years. He was sixty-two and had been in prison since the age of twenty. He was accused of killing two people and was serving two consecutive life sentences. We never had any problems and he was my cellmate for two years. Some people in prison had committed horrible crimes, and those people would be standing right next to you or even sleeping in the metal bunk bed below you. In my cellblock, there were murderers, drug dealers, sex offenders, rapists, repeat DUI offenders, robbers, etc. The list just goes on and on. You probably think all people in prison are bad, but that is not true. There are good people responsible for committing crimes as a result of terrible choices made that, in some way, are related to alcohol or drugs.

The Inmate Speaking Program helped me change the direction of my life. This was a good choice that had good consequences. I finally believed in a cause and knew that I had a course to pursue. I was involved in something positive and I did not care what anyone else thought. Usually, deep inside, I would worry about what others thought, but not in this case. I knew in my heart I was doing the right thing and I was going to follow through with my belief. I need to remember this the next time I am caught in a tough situation. If you know in your gut what is right, don't worry what anyone might say or think about you. Follow through with your belief.

The process, at times, was not pleasant and was quite often frustrating. Deputies from different counties would sign me out and retain temporary custody of me each time I left prison to speak. They would put leg shackles and handcuffs on me, put me in the back of a police car, and then put me on display at schools for students to see, judge, and hear my story. I knew many people were looking down on me, but I would stand there with the chains on and pour my emotions out on stage, describing the pain I caused in so many lives. I was responsible for killing two people and ruining countless lives. My goal was to have others see what my life was like to prevent them from enduring tough consequences from bad choices, especially if they involved alcohol.

Once the other prisoners knew what I was in prison for and what I was trying to do, they accepted it and most supported it. The majority of people in prison do not want others to experience incarceration, addiction to drugs and alcohol, or feel the endless guilt and pain day after day from an irreversible mistake.

When a person is caught in the snares of the prison system, it is ugly. Statistics tell us that almost fifty percent of convicts released from prison return to prison within three years. That is a scary statistic and it reminds me just how easy it is to return back to that nightmare. When you are a convicted felon, life becomes harder and you lose opportunities.

The abuse of alcohol and drugs typically leads to other crimes. These criminal acts can easily result in prison time. Some estimates indicate that over eighty percent of the prison population was under the influence of or possessed drugs or alcohol while committing their crime.

I remember meeting another inmate who was truly a good person. His nickname is Six Nine, because he was six feet, nine inches tall. His real name is John. Like I mentioned before, there are good people in prison. The only thing separating you from them is one bad choice. Six Nine was incarcerated for the same charges as mine, two counts of vehicular homicide by DUI. However, his situation was a little different. He did not hit another car. He dodged a construction barrel and rolled his vehicle, killing the two passengers inside: his cousin, who was his best friend, and his girlfriend. His DUI is because he had traces of weed (marijuana) in his system. Because of a joint, he spent eight years in prison. Driving under the influence is unacceptable, whether it is alcohol or drugs (prescription pills, weed, cocaine, meth, ice, ecstasy, etc.). Food for thought: bad people are not the only ones who go to prison. Good people who make bad choices go to prison too.

I was in several prisons, including the one where I was locked in the cell for twenty-three hours a day. I want to share what a day in the life of a prisoner is like.

The last prison I was housed in had a two-man cell that was 7' x 12' with a sink, a toilet, a locker box, and a metal bunk bed with a thin mat to lie on. There was no privacy and you didn't get to choose your cellmate. I had a few pretty bad ones. I had to tolerate them, but I did not like it. The cell was small and very uncomfortable. During the night, if you had to use the restroom, you had to sit down right next to your bunkmate and handle your business. Being locked in the cell was miserable.

We were locked in our cells overnight and sometimes for short periods during the day. Once the cell doors opened early in the morning, we would prepare for chow call (breakfast/lunch/dinner). After eating the slop, the correctional officers in charge of our unit or cellblock would need to count us. When correctional officers tell you to do something, you better do it or else you face consequences like being sent to solitary confinement. Once count cleared (making sure every inmate is accounted for), we had to go to our detail or prepare for inspection. Details were jobs like picking up trash, cleaning showers and toilets, mowing grass, etc. Inspection was when the warden (the boss of the prison), correctional officers, and administrators would walk into cellblocks to make sure everyone's beds were made and the cellblock was clean. A failed inspection meant restrictions for the whole unit, such as loss of store, recreation, or last to chow.

Chow call! Lunch began. After lunch there was another count by officers. Then, we would return to our work detail. After four o'clock in the afternoon, most work details were over and people started returning to their assigned cellblocks. Convicts might go out to the yard to work out and do some recreational activity, but the yard could also be a very dangerous place. You never knew what to expect on the yard.

Chow call! Dinner was served. We ate garbage, but had to be thankful to get any food. The evening time consisted of count time and a time for prisoners to wind down. For example, some played cards, watched television, read books, wrote letters, or worked out. Playing cards and watching television does not sound too bad, but cards eventually led to a big fight or argument, and television (trick box) would spark off some of the worst incidents, like stabbings. It was hard to agree on a station even when the stations were very limited. You had a bunch of bullies arguing about what to watch. Get in the middle of that mess, and you could wake up with a shank in your back.

Next is the fun part. You get to do it all over again, the same routine day after day and night after night. Correctional officers always called you "inmate" or "convict" and told you what to do, when to do it, and how to do it. Many times I wanted to say no, but I had to follow the rules. If not, there were consequences, such as being dragged to the hole in handcuffs, which only made the situation worse. Then, you were plagued with the fact you had to constantly look over your shoulder wondering what might happen next. You continued to think of how much you missed life outside of prison. This is a dark, depressing, and emotionally draining environment filled with negativity.

Chapter 8
Paroled

Parole from prison came on August 5, 2009. For 3,117 days, I lived behind bars, concrete, and razor wire. At this point, a new phase of my sentence began: parole, and later probation. I reported to the parole office in Conyers, Georgia on the same day as I was released. When I was called back to meet with my parole officer, the experience was similar to being summoned into a courtroom. The rules of parole were explained and the consequences for violations were emphatically made clear. Being sent back to the chain gang is always looming while on parole. The rules were extensive. I would have to pay a supervision fee each month, report to the parole office monthly, request permission before leaving the state, and have my driver's license suspended indefinitely or until the judge ruled otherwise. I was also required to return to the crash site on April 11 each year to place flowers there in memory of the two people I killed. Did I mention that this stage of my sentence does not end until April 9, 2031? One bad choice or a few thoughtless choices and my rear end will be right back in jail.

The parole office is a crazy place. There are all kinds of people waiting to be seen by their assigned officer. Some days, the wait could be up to two hours. There are parolees who have not learned to follow the rules, and parole officers will handcuff those individuals and a sheriff deputy will take them straight back to jail. Everyone waiting to be seen is visibly stressed out. Many of the felons cannot find jobs, and if they do not work they are in jeopardy of being sent back to prison.

Living life as a convicted felon is incredibly difficult. The public expects parolees to violate the rules or to be convicted of another crime. There is a certain expectation of failure for most. Add to that the baggage of being an ex-con, and a lot of parolees just give up. Opportunities for failure are far more plentiful than for success. Because I chose to drink and drive, I lost the privilege to drive. I am harshly judged by most people, even after being judged and sentenced in the courtroom. Certain jobs are no longer available to me because of my background. Doing hard time is not limited to prison.

During the eight and a half years I spent in prison, so much had changed. I was honestly ignorant to the basic things of the free world. I had much to learn.

On top of everything else, I still had to deal with the parole office. Parole officers visit your home or place of employment to make sure you are doing what you have stated. They do not trust their parolees until they have proven themselves. If they catch you lying, you can go back to prison. Parole officers are not in the business of being overly tolerant. You either follow their rules or live your life by way of the penitentiary's revolving door. Just because you have a good job lined up and are making money does not mean you have arrived on Easy Street. You will be tested over and over to make sure you are mentally ready to exist in society.

After three years on parole, the parole office recognized my good behavior. The accountability I had exhibited proved that I was a changed person. If you do the right things in life and follow the rules life can get better, but it takes patience and hard work to earn trust. When I want to travel out of state, I have to acquire a travel permit or risk violating my parole. A parole officer can still come to my house and check on me anytime he or she thinks a visit might be necessary. They can do that until my sentence is completed in 2031. My absolute freedom is in bondage until that time expires because of the choice I made many years ago.

Site of Crash

Chapter 9
Living Life After Causing Death

Parole is demanding and probation is challenging, but nothing is more difficult than living with the guilt of killing two innocent people. All this pain because I wanted to have a few drinks and hurry to another party. That was stupid, selfish, and ignorant, and it is a choice I will regret for the rest of my life.

The victims' family is forever changed and so is mine. I can never undo what has been done, and I will always carry in my heart the knowledge that I killed someone's wonderful parents and grandparents.

Some statistics tell us that one in three people will be involved in an alcohol related crash.

Students in high school and college are sometimes blinded by the false belief that being under the influence of drugs and alcohol does not adversely affect their abilities behind the wheel. Everyone knows that is false. Multiple reports show that approximately 600,000 college students are unintentionally injured while under the influence of alcohol every year. Any person maintaining the attitude that they can drive when they are drunk or high will ultimately pay a huge price.

In my current neighborhood, I have only been able to tell a few people that I was in prison. I am ashamed of the person I once was and of the choices I made.

When you are labeled a convicted felon, seeking employment becomes very difficult. Imagine how a typical interview is conducted.

"Well, Mr. Sandy, what did you do between April 10, 2001, and August 5, 2009? That is a long time to be out of work."

Then there is also the question that could very well be a deal breaker. "Mr. Sandy, have you ever been convicted of a felony?"

Of course my response could only be the truth. "Yes, sir, I was in prison for almost eight and a half years. I was drinking and driving one evening and caused a horrific car crash. My action resulted in the deaths of two innocent people."

"I understand, Mr. Sandy. Thank you for your honesty, but we have several other people who have more suitable qualifications for the available position. We will keep your application on file. Good luck!"

Have I mentioned the details of my first doctor's appointment after my parole? I needed to see a doctor for help with a staph infection I had contracted while in prison. It was Methicillin-resistant Staphylococcus aureus (MRSA). As soon as the physician started asking questions, I knew I had just entered an arena that was going to be difficult to navigate.

The doctor asked, "Which doctor treated you previously, and can I get a copy of your medical records?

I responded, "Well, Doc, that could be complicated. I have been in prison for the last eight and a half years."

The doctor said, "Okay, let's get you treated and also, let's test you for HIV."

Then she wrote a bunch of stuff down in her chart. Thankfully, my tests came back negative and everything was fine, but the experience was humiliating. People assume that when you come out of prison you automatically have some dreaded disease. The truth of the matter is that a lot of people do leave prison with some kind of medical condition that they did not have when they entered the system. Prison is confined and dirty, and there are any number of contagious diseases floating around. Because of budget constraints and lack of concern, medical care is limited. The situation is more than a little frightening.

I am writing this book in a Starbucks coffee shop. That is my big hang out. I enjoy the atmosphere, and I notice a lot of people are working hard to complete their daily tasks or networking to achieve their future goals. The coffee shop is not close, so getting there can be a bit challenging because I do not have a driver's license. In order to get from one place to another, I walk, rely on others for a ride, or call a taxi. Today, my mom dropped me off on her way to work, and my friend, Lincoln Nunnally, is going to take some time away from work to give me a ride home. Making new friends as a convicted felon is tough. I choose positive people to be in my inner circle but it will take a lot of patience to rebuild my life. There was a time when I had many friends, but that is not the case anymore. I am just lucky to be out of prison.

Attempting to cope with my actions from many years ago is a daily struggle. I am on medication for depression and I still seek the guidance of a counselor. Overcoming the effects of years in prison is problematic, but living with the consequences of my earlier actions is traumatic. Even if I had not been sentenced to prison, I would still have many obstacles to face. Please understand, living life after causing death is a life sentence of consequences. When I learned that release from prison was in the near future, I was able to finally see light at the end of the tunnel. The opportunity was within reach to prove to my family and all my supporters that I was going to do something positive with my life.

Several people within my family will never know me on the other side of prison. They will never know whether I was able to overcome the consequences of my bad choices. Four of those family members are my grandparents. They all died while I was in prison. Life cannot be relived, as mistakes cannot be erased.

My dad's side of the family did not want my grandmother to know I was in prison, so they kept that fact hidden for over seven years. Grandma Sophie was told that I worked on an oil rig in Alaska and hardly ever had time to visit. I was never able to write to her since all outgoing mail from the prison is stamped. Looking back, I am sure I could have found some way to write a letter without her knowing about my incarceration, but I did not know what to say. I was in prison and was plagued by negative thoughts. I respected my family's wishes. Everyone was afraid she would worry herself to death if she found out I was in a penitentiary. My grandma should not have to suffer because of my choice. My grandma, Sophie, died before I was paroled from prison.

In addition to my grandparents, I also lost another important family member while in prison. Thursday, November 22, 2007, was Thanksgiving. I was able to receive a visit from my family. I had just found out that I was getting out sooner than expected, and as a family we had a lot for which to be thankful. Dad made the long drive from Tampa, Florida to Atlanta, Georgia to see me. He traveled to the prison with Mom, my sister, Angela, and my nephew, Christopher. I was truly grateful that they were willing to drive to the prison and spend time with me on Thanksgiving. Who wants to spend their holiday in a prison? There were almost a thousand prisoners housed there, and my guess is that only fifteen percent of the population got a visit. I was very thankful for the love and support of my family.

My family was well-versed in the routine of entering a prison for visitation. They had to pass through the metal detector and the mechanical doors that crashed behind them. Everyone was told where to sit. As I entered the visitation room, there was also a routine. I was escorted to the bathroom, searched for any contraband, and instructed that I could hug everyone one time. Once seated, I was to stay put, unless I needed to use the restroom. Even then, permission had to be granted by a correctional officer.

That day brings up difficult memories. Thinking back, I recalled being a teenager and thinking I had life all figured out. I thought my parents were just oblivious to what it was like to be a teenager or young adult. I was so hardheaded. I stopped listening to my parents and started doing whatever I wanted to do. I thought I knew what was best for me. That attitude really drove a wedge between my dad and me. He was tired of dealing with my attitude, so we just avoided each other during my late teens and early twenties. What happened next was my decision to drink and drive and the horrific results that followed. Dad had tried to warn me that something like that could happen if I was not careful. If I had only listened, then I would not be responsible for taking the lives of two wonderful people.

During visitation on Thanksgiving, I remember Dad getting up to go to the vending machines. He was buying everything. By the time he brought over this ridiculous amount of food, I felt as though we must have looked like the biggest hobo family on the planet. To tell the truth, Dad just wanted me to feel like we were having a Thanksgiving dinner together as a family. If I could not be home for Thanksgiving, then he was going to do his best to bring home to me. It's hard to accomplish that in prison, but my dad wanted the best for me. While I was doing my time in prison, he stood by my side the whole way and we became closer than we had ever been before. I just knew that when I got out of prison we were going to have some good times together; fishing, cooking out, and going to football games. I was going to be given the opportunity to prove to him that I had genuinely changed my course in life.

Once visitation ended, everyone prepared to leave and we all hugged. I remember Dad and I always had that handshake and man hug. That was something we started while I was in prison. Those embraces felt really good. Dad got into the car with Mom, my sister, Angela, and her son, Christopher. Visiting with family on Thanksgiving had truly been a blessing.

Soon after visitation, my dorm was sent to the chow hall for our Thanksgiving dinner. The vending machine picnic had been a feast compared to what we were being offered; that taste of home had left me in my own harsh reality. After the evening meal, we were sent back to our cellblocks.

Minutes later, a lieutenant came and escorted me from my cell. I asked what was going on, but he had nothing to say. I thought I could be in trouble for something, but I knew I had not done anything wrong. In prison, though, some prisoners play dirty and ruthless games. They might plant a shank under your bunk or some drugs in your cell just to get you locked up. We would call them haters because they would be mad that you got a visit and they did not.

I noticed the officer was taking me back to the multi-purpose room. I thought this was odd. I peered through the glass doors and saw my mom standing in what had been the visitation area. She was crying uncontrollably. I attempted to turn around. I did not want to enter those doors. I knew something terrible had to have happened for my mom to be allowed to come back into the prison. The lieutenant was a good man, and proved that again by assisting me into the room. Mom sat down with me and told me that my dad had a massive heart attack just down the road from the prison. Mom's cell service would not connect. My sister tried CPR, but all they could do was watch my dad die right there on the side of the road.

That moment was the worst experience of my life in prison. It was difficult to accept the last time my dad saw me was in the penitentiary. I did not get to help my family make the arrangements for his funeral and burial. By accident, Mom and Angela had my dad buried in the same cemetery as the King family (the two people I killed). For several years, I could not even visit Dad's gravesite because of the guilt I carried. I am doing better now because I know I have to move forward.

Chapter 10
My Mission and Goals

My decisions have caused way too much pain in the lives of entirely too many people. Now there is a debt to be paid, and my mission is to pay it forward. Individuals can learn from my mistakes without having to endure the regret. I want to better communicate the consequences of thoughtless decisions and selfish behavior. Going to a party while in high school and drinking to impress a particular person or peer group is poor judgement. After reaching that point, a person will start to believe that the only way to have fun is to drink. There is more to life than attempting to exist in an altered state of consciousness. Everyone needs to come to the understanding that having fun while being sober is far more memorable and nowhere near as costly.

Teens die all the time from drunk driving, alcohol poisoning, and drug overdoses. That is not living your life to the fullest. College students make choices all the time while under the influence of alcohol and drugs that ruin their educational opportunities, athletic dreams, or future careers. College is intended to be a growing experience, so young adults should be responsible and plan ahead to guard an enriching college experience. Those years for me were spent in a Georgia state prison because I was irresponsible and my plan was not purposeful. Compare the two paths available. One course of action prepares you for a life of opportunities. The other separates you from any chances of being prepared for what life has to offer. Is that a difficult choice to make?

Even through the heartache and guilt, I know I must press forward. Setting and accomplishing goals is a key to living a fulfilling life. This is advice that everyone should follow. I wanted to speak in an effort to help others and I wanted to start volunteering for the same reason; both goals accomplished. I wanted to be married and have a family; goal accomplished. I want to travel to forty-eight states (might not be able to travel to Hawaii or Alaska due to being on parole); a goal in progress. I wanted to be able to drive again; finally, done! I want to be a better person; will always be working on that. Unfortunately, my goals and dreams are always overshadowed by my poor choice. Do not rob yourself of ambitions and dreams by living in regret.

Set goals, achieve goals, and dream big! I believe in this generation of young people. Now is the time for this generation to begin believing in themselves. BELIEVE!

Chapter 11
What Have I Learned?

With almost half of my life behind me, I have learned…

What I could have learned while in high school, I did not. I should have not only heard, but listened to what was being taught. Instead of trying to live in the moment, I could have been building on those moments with the essentials that would have provided the foundation for a purposeful future. Alternatively, I have been taught by the school of hard knocks, which is far more costly. Though my high school days are behind me, my future from this point forward has not yet been written, and that which lies ahead will be built on the bedrock of thoughtful choices.

My circle of friends should be determined by factors of contribution and not by popularity. The question, "Is this individual going to positively contribute to my life or am I going to have the opportunity to guide his or her life?" needs to be asked prior to choosing friends. Accountability will be a characteristic inherent to the circle of friends to which I belong. Everyone should be duly concerned with the welfare of one another, and not worried about what may or may not be the social norm.

Driving is not only a privilege, but is also an awesome responsibility. Yes, a car or truck is basically a means of transportation, but that same vehicle operated while impaired (under the influence) or distracted (texting) can easily become a means of destruction or death. Being irresponsible with this privilege can dramatically drive home the undeniable truth that life is fragile, and violating that truism will have devastating consequences.

Making choices is an unavoidable practice of life, but making poor choices is not only irresponsible, it is also selfish. When evaluating my options, I have a responsibility to primarily consider the well-being of others before giving notice to my needs and wants. People are affected by the choices I make.

My self-worth is best determined by the quality of my relationships with family and friends. This should never be taken for granted or in any way abused. Some goals that I have set regarding these personal assets are to be a better husband to my wife, a better father to my children, a better son to my mother, a better brother to my sister, and a better friend to my friends. If I desire the finer things life has to offer then I must first appreciate that which has lasting value. Relationships that are built on trust, mutual respect, and unconditional love will stand the test of time.

Forgiveness does not mean forgetting, and mistakes cannot be erased. Forgiveness is a form of separation from the offense. I might never receive forgiveness from the victims' family, but forgiveness may be given to me by others, such as my family, friends, and even strangers. Forgiveness is more readily given when evidence is shown that the wrongdoer has committed to making wiser choices. I cannot erase my mistakes but I can change the life patterns that led to those mistakes. Moving forward, no matter how difficult the journey may be, is essential to becoming a better person and contributor to society.

Every day is plagued with the thoughts of living life after causing death. I want to pass on what I have learned. My hope is that others will reflect on their lives and determine the appropriate changes they need to make in order to press forward toward their continued success. If you have allowed yourself to get derailed from what you know is right, it is time to get back on track and make something of yourself. I remember those days of not wanting to live. Life has been made difficult by my choices, but I do understand that I now have another opportunity at life on Earth. I have learned that life is about helping others. My family, faith, friends, and opportunity to help others are what keep my life full of purpose.

Please put thought into your decisions and make responsible choices. Please do not live a life of regret.

Eric Krug's Story

Chapter 1
The Beginning

This book is the story of more than one person.

April 11, 1997, was Eric's twenty-first birthday. His celebration was to begin at midnight; the beginning of Eric's legal drinking age. Eric had played in a college baseball game earlier that day. That was the last time he would ever play baseball.

Eric Joshua Krug was born on April 11, 1976. Yes, April 11. Eric was the youngest of three children, and he grew up with two wonderful parents, Joyce and Jack Krug. Jack Krug was a salesman and Joyce was a housewife who worked tirelessly to meet the needs of their family of five. Jack had to travel often, but always attended both of his sons' games, whether it was football or baseball. Eric's older brother, John, was a very athletic young man. He loved football and eventually played at Rhodes College, where he earned his degree. John has a wonderful wife, Carole, and two precious children, Jake and Connor.

Eric also has an amazing sister, Jennifer. Jennifer was her daddy's little girl, and she did like playing tennis, but was more interested in academics than sports. Eric and Jennifer have always been extremely close and share a special bond. Since Eric was the youngest, John and Jennifer always teased him, because in their eyes, he got everything he wanted. They were your typical siblings, always thinking one was being favored over the other. Jack and Joyce loved them all the same. Their love was not partial.

John and Eric were talented athletes and they made Jack a very proud father. In high school, Eric played both football and baseball, but his love was baseball. Eric was a gifted athlete and student. He was one of those people who never had to study for tests and could breeze right through them. Eric really had the complete package. He was athletic, intelligent, and humorous. He was blessed with family, friends, and, as Eric would joke, "hot girlfriends". Now Eric can only dream of those days. His life is far from normal and more than just a little complicated.

Chapter 2
Living the Dream

In high school, Eric dreamed of playing college baseball and moving on to the big leagues. He was an average teenager with above average aspirations and dreams. Eric was able to move to the next level after high school and he played college baseball at Oglethorpe University in Atlanta, Georgia. He received a scholarship and was excited about the opportunity to play baseball in college. He was living his dream.

During his freshman year, Eric was confronted with a few struggles. What freshman does not get distracted by the new surroundings of college? For the first time in his life, his grades were not perfect. There was no doubt that he was slacking off. Eric was adjusting to college life. After the coaches had a talk with him, Eric tightened the slack and was immediately back on track.

Each year, Eric improved. Everyone commented on his talent. He was a well-rounded player who could hit the ball and field very well. By the time he made it to his junior year, he was voted All-Conference and Defensive MVP. Eric was living in the field of dreams.

Eric was like many college students. He liked to go out and have fun. Sometimes, that fun included drinking with his friends. Eric and his friends really did not see any harm in throwing back a few drinks and doing what many other students were doing around them. However, Eric and his friends now know that a night of fun can quickly turn into a nightmare.

If you ever get to see Eric in person, you will understand. That is why I am assisting in the telling of this tragic and heart-wrenching story, which should be sobering to all who listen.

Chapter 3
Eric's 21st Birthday

The baseball game was played on April 10, 1997. One of Eric's best friends, teammate, and roommate was Tim. Tim's position was third base and Eric's was second base. During the game, Eric and Tim made an incredible double play which won the game for their team. The night was off to a great start!

Jennifer, Eric's sister, had thought about getting her little brother a limo for his 21st birthday celebration, but changed her mind because of the expense and the fact there were plenty of taxis in the area. The college Eric attended was in Atlanta. The amount of people who would go to this area was unbelievable. It was a huge party scene full of bars and clubs.

The game was out of town, so they did not get back to Oglethorpe University until 10:00 pm. The night was not set to begin until midnight. Eric and his friends made a pact to take taxis back to campus, which was the responsible choice.

The night was a typical twenty-one-year-old's celebration. The whole crew was drinking heavily. Eric was slammed a few hours later, and the time came for everyone to go home. Some took cabs and others did not.

Jennifer made a point of putting Eric and his girlfriend into a taxi.

Jen leaned in and said, "I love you."

She walked away and returned to the bar to grab her purse. The plan was for them to meet back at Eric's dorm. Campus was just a short drive from where they had been partying. I am sure many thought that nothing bad could happen.

Right before they drove off, a small group of Eric's friends walked by the taxi. They talked Eric and his girlfriend, Marie, into getting out and riding back to campus with them. That was not part of Jen's or Eric's plan. Eric was not in any condition to make that call, but he stumbled out of the taxi anyway. He was a college student and did not want to waste the little money he had. Plus, he wanted to be with his friends. These were his friends, and he was not going to tell them no. What a huge mistake.

Reflecting on that evening, one word or action could have changed the outcome of that horrific night. If Eric had not given in to peer pressure and had not gotten out of the taxi, or if his friends had simply gotten into the cab, as agreed on earlier, then the ending of this story would be much different.

Chapter 4
The Crash

The car into which Eric climbed belonged to Tim's girlfriend, Missy. She was drunk, but felt she could easily drive the short distance back to campus. Nobody took her keys, and this mistake was compounded when others got into the car with her. In their blurred consciousness, they trusted her judgement. Bad idea.

They drove onto campus, passed security, and veered off to the right. This road was small, lined with trees on both sides, and led to the dorms. All the roads on campus were narrow and meant to be driven on carefully. Going against what was intended, the driver flew down the road, driving between thirty-five and forty-five miles per hour. As she came around a small turn, about 300 yards from their final destination, Missy lost control and her Jetta flew into the trees on the right side of the road. The car crashed into a couple of trees before coming to a complete stop.

Tim was sitting in the back seat. Unfortunately, he was the only one not wearing a seatbelt. He was sitting in the middle between two people, and the crash had enough impact to launch him from the back seat, head first, into the dashboard. The results were horrific. A resident assistant at the university had to hold his head together. Tim's skull split open from the impact. There are not words in my vocabulary to describe that type of injury. Tim was rushed to the hospital and clung to life, but his injuries were too severe. Tim died ten hours later.

Eric was in the passenger seat. The weather was nice out, so he had the window rolled down and his arm and hand were resting on the edge. When the car crashed into the trees, Eric's arm was severed at the elbow, barely staying attached. His bones were completely crushed from his elbow all the way down to his hand. It was his right arm; his throwing arm. The doctors thought the arm would need to be amputated, but thankfully, they saved it. However, his right arm would never be the same. Eric's arm does not rotate correctly and he cannot fully open his hand or extend his fingers. He has to sleep with an open brace on his arm to allow his fingers to extend slightly. He uses that hand simply as a clamp. Something as natural as throwing a baseball is now an impossibility.

I wish I could tell you that this was the extent of Eric's injuries as a result of the crash. His arm is minor in comparison to his other injuries. Eric's head hit the windshield before it hit a tree. His head slammed into that tree traveling at a speed of thirty-five to forty-five miles per hour. His skull had two fractures. Eric suffered a closed head injury, complicated by a brain stem injury and a broken neck. He fell into a deep coma at the scene. Eric also had bones all over his body that were broken and injured. He was near death, and the doctors said Eric was only breathing a few breaths per minute when admitted. Look at your watch and attempt to breathe once every fifteen seconds. It's crazy and very scary to imagine. Eric probably should had died, but his age and athletic condition kept him alive.

Missy, the drunk driver, did not suffer any serious injuries.

One young, wonderful man's life was cut short. Eric had lost his best friend, Tim. Eric was injured for life. Give serious thought to the fact that Missy killed her boyfriend, a consequence she will endure for the rest of her life. Everyone in that car paid an emotional or physical price for choosing to get into a car with someone who had been drinking.

THE STORMY PETREL

Volume 72, Issue 11   Above and Beyond Oglethorpe University

OU mourns student's death in car accide

by Catherine Borck
News Editor

A wind-whipped silhece rushed over the empty baseball field onto Hermance Stadium's largest crowd of the year. The crowd had gathered to mourn the loss of Timothy R. Crowley, who died after sustaining injuries in an automobile accident on April 11. The Oglethorpe community is hiring statistic from the death of the star baseball player and died as was undergoing surgery.

This season Crowley's batting average was an OU-record .434 with 33 RBIs, 18 more than the previous OU-extended Crowley has been nominated for the Coastal Academic All-Region Team along with John Doyle. Crowley's batting averages according to Dunn Scheglhauser type Like Appling's an Oglethorpe all-time short-stop from 1927.

"He was the best player Oglethorpe had, we because, he was the most talented.

Campus crash results in death, 2 serious injuries

by Catherine Borck
News Editor

A car accident occurred at approximately 2:20 a.m. Friday, April 11 on campus resulting in the death of 1 passenger and left 2 others seriously injured. Senior Timothy R. Crowley died at DeKalb Medical Center later Friday after sustaining serious head and lung injuries. Four other Oglethorpe students, Melissa Roedersheimer, Marie Lu King and David Brooks were in the accident.

in serious condition in a medically-induced coma. He was also fighting a viral infection and pneumonia but has shown signs of improvement.

Brooks sustained a broken leg and was taken to Dunwoody Medical Center along with Biro.

According to the police report, the driver of the automobile apparently lost control of the vehicle while driving on the private drive that circles campus. The car left the roadway and struck a

---

Campus crash results in 1 death, 2 serious injuries

by Catherine Borck
News Editor

A car accident occurred at approximately 2:20 a.m. Friday, April 11 on campus resulting in the death of 1 passenger and left 2 others seriously injured. Senior Timothy R. Crowley died at DeKalb Medical Center later Friday after sustaining serious head and lung injuries. Four other Oglethorpe students, Melissa Roedersheimer, Marie

in serious condition in a medically-induced coma. He was also fighting a viral infection and pneumonia but has shown signs of improvement.

Brooks sustained a broken leg and was taken to Dunwoody Medical Center along with Biro.

According to the police report, the driver of the automobile apparently lost control of the vehicle while driving on the private drive that circles campus. The car left the roadway and struck a

Chapter 5
Life-Changing Injury

Eric's severe head trauma caused his brain to swell, injuring every lobe on his brain. He was in a comatose state for over a year. He did not blink his eyes, move his hands, talk, or wiggle his toes for several months. There was simply no response. Joyce, Jack, John, and Jennifer did everything possible to try to get a reaction from him. Jennifer would crawl in the bed with him, talk to him for hours, and play his music. She tried everything to get him to wake up. Eric just lay there and was not responsive to any stimuli. There were many nights the Krug family felt hopeless and helpless. They just wanted Eric to wake up and tell them he was all right, but that was never going to happen because Eric was not all right. He was hurt badly.

All of Eric's friends visited him in the hospital, but they could only sit and wait to see if he was going to wake up. They tried to talk to him, but Eric was unresponsive. Eric's beautiful girlfriend, Marie, was scared to death. Her life was deteriorating with each passing month. The Krugs and Marie's parents were beginning to notice that she was not the same girl; her life was falling apart. The Krugs had to step in and ask Marie to return home to her parents and move forward with her life. I know this sounds cruel, but another life was being ruined, and they did not want that for this sweet girl. There was a chance Eric's brain was so damaged that he would be in a vegetative state for the rest of his life even if he did wake from the coma; a truth many could not bear to think about. Eric was supposed to be a baseball player, graduate college with a degree in business, and be successful. Eric's family would continue to ask themselves why something like this happened to their child.

Eric's body was constantly fighting off infections. He had life-threatening staph infections, bouts with pneumonia, and numerous complications that could have easily taken his life during those endless months of hospital confinement. This once all-star athlete who was almost six feet tall and weighed 185 lbs. had shriveled to an unhealthy 130 lbs.

Early on, the doctors were at a point of preparing the family for Eric's death. Eric's mom would not give thought to any of those notions, and knew her son was still fighting. She prayed to God day and night and knew in her heart that Eric would wake up.

Finally, after many months, those prayers were answered. Eric opened his eyes. He did not sit up in bed, move his arms, or stand on his feet. Eric simply opened his eyes and stared out into space. That, in itself, was a miracle. The family was ecstatic, but feared what the future held. Eric had actually just entered another stage of his coma, but it was at least something for which to be hopeful.

Traumatic Brain Injury (TBI) was the diagnosis, and even after Eric fully emerged from the coma, he would face numerous challenges.

The rate and extent of recovery for those afflicted by TBI varies from person to person. Understanding how the brain functions normally is still a mystery, so one can only imagine the difficulties that are faced after suffering a severe brain injury. Doctors do know the brain finds different pathways to work around the damaged areas, but those detours might limit or alter the way an individual might think, act, or even look. TBI is complex, and there needs to be more research on it and more resources for those individuals affected by this kind of injury.

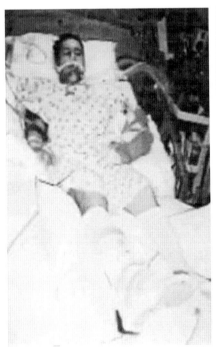 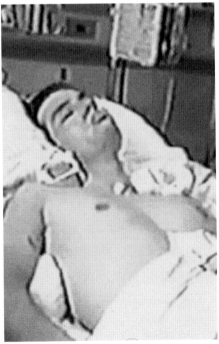

Chapter 6
The Nursing Home

The next stage of Eric's TBI recovery affected not only Eric, but the entire Krug family. In July of 1997, three months after the crash, the doctors ordered the Krug family to put Eric in a nursing home. The doctors felt as if Eric could not recover any further than his current state of being. Those who knew and loved Eric felt that the doctors were asking them to do something that his family was not yet willing to do, which was to give up on Eric's recovery.

The doctors told the Krug family that caring for Eric would be too difficult, and he would be better off in a nursing home. The doctors knew how demanding it would be to care for Eric, and a lot of families simply cannot handle the daily challenges of caring for someone with a brain injury. Eric could not do anything for himself. Someone had to bathe and dress him, feed him through a feeding tube that was inserted into his stomach, and administer all his medications throughout the day. His adult diapers would need to be changed regularly, and his body would need to be turned to various positions during the day, keeping him from having skin bedsores. This was a full time job. Several trained nurses had to be available to care for Eric's injured body, as he was still physically fragile during those months. This was not an easy task for any one family to attempt alone in a home setting.

Nursing homes are a very practical place for many people, but Eric's mom, dad, and sister believed that Eric would receive the care and attention that he most needed while staying at the family home. On top of the medical necessities, Eric needed to be mentally and physically stimulated so as to excel in his progress. They wanted him freed from the clutches of the coma, and the nursing home seemed to be a step in a different direction. This was not only a physically strenuous undertaking, but an emotional one as well.

As in most nursing homes, there are certain limitations, and the family could not accept the treatment offered to their son. Eric's family stayed with him day and night for five straight days. They maintained a watchful eye over his care. Eric's mother worked tirelessly to find a way to get Eric moved out of that nursing home. This was an extremely difficult task and was heavy on the minds and hearts of the entire Krug family. After a tremendous amount of agony, they moved Eric out of the nursing home and into a new hospital that would promote and encourage his continued recovery.

Several weeks prior, the family had made efforts to have him admitted into the Scottish Rite Hospital in Atlanta, Georgia, but was denied. Finally, a wonderful staff member at that hospital, who will remain anonymous, gave the green light to have Eric admitted. Scottish Rite is a children's hospital, so Eric was right at the cut-off age of twenty-one. This hospital was amazing. The doctors, nurses, and therapists were making a huge difference for Eric and his family. After several months of dedicated, wonderful care and rehabilitation therapy, Eric's physical condition was now listed as stable and enabled him to be moved again. This time he went home.

APR 1 1998

100

Chapter 7
Going Home

The process of moving home was demanding for the Krug family. First, Eric was moved to his parents' house. The living room on the main floor was turned into Eric's bedroom. Unfortunately, the house was two stories and did not have a full bath on the main level, which complicated the situation. The family had to drag Eric upstairs every time he needed to take a bath. After a couple of months, Eric had to be moved to his sister's one-story ranch-style house, where he would reside in the dining room. Neither of these houses was handicap accessible and refurbishing a home would cost thousands of dollars. They could not handle such a financial burden because of the hospital bills stacked on the kitchen counter. The Krugs would simply make do with what they could afford. Since Jennifer's home was all on one level, it was much easier to get Eric to a bathroom. A typical bath routine would take at least two hours and would be exhausting for everyone involved. Caring for Eric was a huge undertaking. Eric was still in a semi-comatose state and could not hold himself up. He was basically a limp body. Eric was this way as a twenty-one- and twenty-two-year-old kid, who was once a stellar athlete. Now he could no longer care for himself. They would lay him down in the dining room to change his diaper, which was embarrassing to Eric. Jennifer was mortified that she had to do this for her brother, but it had to be done, and she would ultimately do anything for him.

As time went on, Eric was able to be tied to a chair to start training his body to sit up. At this point, he was beginning to slowly emerge from his comatose condition. Since Eric could not talk, no one knew if he was capable of communicating. He would have flashing moments, but it was very difficult to get Eric to retain any information. He simply had to relearn everything. At first, he could only nod his head, but still had a blank stare most of the time. Eventually, they made a huge card with letters, numbers, and words. Eric's vision was altered from his injuries to the point of where he was seeing double and occasionally having blurred vision. When they showed this card to Eric, he was able to slowly spell with his left hand pointing to letters to form words. His right hand still did not work. It was amazing he was actually learning how to communicate again. This was a much-needed milestone for Eric and the whole family. Communication had to be kept simple, but it was at least a starting point.

The family stayed at Jennifer's house for almost two years. Then, Eric's parents had a house built that was handicap accessible. This was a must for Eric to rehabilitate and function. Eric had to be in a wheelchair, and was told he probably would not walk again. He still could not talk because of the injury to his brain. Eric was in continual physical and speech therapy. It was his new way of life. Eric was working very hard, but his progress was slow.

This had a huge impact on Eric's family. Joyce and Jack did not know how to handle this new life. Eric had traumatic brain injury and would never be the same. Life was completely different and very complicated now. They could barely get out of bed some days, but had to in order to face the jobs in front of them, such as caring for their son or paying the mounting hospital bills. Eventually, Jennifer quit her job, sold her house, and moved home to care for her family. She had to pull everyone together, and that is exactly what she did. Jennifer was dealing with a lot, too. She regretted not renting a limo and she felt at fault, but it was not her fault. Jennifer put Eric and his girlfriend in the taxi. They unfortunately made the choice to get out of the cab.

Eric continued with his rehab and started feeding himself and getting around the house in his wheelchair. We call his wheelchair his "prison on wheels". He still could not talk, but his memory was getting better, so he could spell a little better on his board. Soon, he was able to slowly type his words on a computer and was able to communicate better with his family.

Eric's appearance most definitely changed with his brain injury. I hate pointing that out because it probably bothers Eric, but it is important to share. Eric did not look the same and lost a lot of muscle because he could not use his body the way he did playing college baseball. Eric was very aware of his injuries and had to deal with a lot of anger issues and suicidal thoughts. Life continued to get harder for Eric.

Since the crash, Eric has made improvements. He no longer needs adult diapers and he can do the basics by himself; eat, shower, shave, and get dressed. He still uses his wheelchair most of the time, but he can use his walker for short distances. We are waiting for him to walk without it, but that dream might not happen. If Eric falls, he cannot catch himself, so he might break an arm, shoulder, or collarbone. This has happened before, so Eric knows from experience.

Chapter 8
Eric's Friends and Girlfriend

There were a ton of Eric's friends at the hospital, but when he came home, things started to change. Eric's friends did not like seeing Eric in his condition, so they started visiting less often. Now, he has a few old friends that get together with him once or twice a year. It is difficult for everyone, but especially for Eric. Imagine living with a brain injury that has imprisoned you in a very complicated body and resulted in you basically losing all your friends. Sad and lonely. Those are the only words to describe Eric's situation. His former girlfriend, Marie, has not been able to come back to visit him. This event forever changed her life, too.

Mistakes were made by everyone on the night of the crash, but that was no excuse for Eric's friend choosing to drive her car. That night, she took on the responsibility for all the people who entered her vehicle. Whether or not she will ever admit that, it is the truth. When you let people ride in your car, you assume responsibility for those people. If you drive too fast, text while you drive, or drink and drive, you are responsible for anything that happens to your passengers. Risking the lives of your friends or innocent bystanders is selfish and irresponsible.

Just because mistakes were made by Eric and his friends does not mean he did not have great friends. Eric had wonderful friends, but they had a very hard time coping with the results from that horrific night. Those same friends just could not handle seeing Eric in his new body. I know his family was disappointed in some of his friends, but this whole situation was hard for everyone to deal with. Friends can move on, but family cannot. Eric's friends, new and old, and his family love Eric for who he is and what he stands for, but seeing him navigate his challenged body is hard for all to witness. Eric is not mad at anyone for not visiting more often. He has a huge heart and is very understanding. I did not know the old Eric, but I respect and love the Eric I see now.

Eric lost so much by choosing to get out of that taxi and get into a car driven by a drunk driver. His dream of marrying his girlfriend vanished, and everything normal in his life changed forever.

Although Eric does not get to see his old friends as much as he would want to, he does have a friend that he met several years ago named Heather. They e-mail often, and she comes by and picks Eric up a few times a year to go out to dinner, a movie, or a Braves game. Heather is a sweet girl, and I am glad she has made time in her life to make Eric a happier person. Eric probably e-mails her a hundred times a day, but can you blame him? He doesn't have any other girls e-mailing him or any other friends stopping by to say hi. Seriously, in

Eric's speaking presentations, he is not shy to tell you he has not been on a real date since April 11, 1997. Can you imagine that?

Chapter 9
Walking Big Sister Down the Aisle

Thankfully, this chapter shares some positive accomplishments. Eric's sister, Jennifer, met a wonderful man named Harold. Jennifer really needed some comfort in her life and someone to lean on. In 2000, Jennifer and Harold decided to get married. Finally, something good was happening in the Krug family. Eric, Jennifer, and Harold wanted to surprise everyone by having Eric walk his sister down the aisle at her wedding. Eric worked very hard at rehab to even get to a point where this could be achievable. Eric wanted to do this more than anything, and his hard work, desire, and commitment paid off.

When the wedding day arrived, Eric was ready. Now, please understand, Eric could not walk by himself. He was seriously injured, so even if he could do it with a walker, it would be a miracle. The music started playing for Jennifer to walk down the aisle. Everyone turned around and, with complete shock, saw Eric walking his sister down the aisle. Everybody was in tears and could not believe it. Eric was walking his sister down the aisle! Amazingly, Eric really did it and you could see the pure joy on his face. You can see it in the picture provided in this book. He actually did it. Wow!

Eric even danced with people at the reception. I was told he never had much rhythm to begin with, so his dancing skills had not been affected too much. Three years had passed, and finally some progress. This was an accomplished goal the whole family could enjoy.

Chapter 10
It's Still My Life

This is a special chapter.

Eric's injuries prevented him from having a job, so he just sat around the house all day. He still could not talk without adaptive equipment, get around without a wheelchair or walker, and he needed someone nearby most of the time.

In 2005, an officer from DeKalb County, Georgia wanted to meet Eric and his mom, Joyce. He had an idea – one that Joyce was not crazy about at first. DeKalb County does a Ghost Out program (pre-prom activities) for their high school students. They wanted Eric and Joyce to share their story and be a part of the Ghost Out program, however, that meant Joyce would have to do all the talking. She did not think she could do it, but the officer really helped out. He helped them work on their speech, and created a powerful DVD depicting Eric's life before and after his crash. It is called "It's Still My Life". You can watch this video on YouTube by searching for "It's Still My Life" with Eric Krug. The officer was a blessing and really gave them some purpose in life, especially Eric. Eric and Joyce have been sharing their story on a regular basis since 2005, and have spoken to hundreds of thousands of teens all across the state of Georgia. Joyce is Eric's pillar of strength and together they change lives every year. It is truly inspirational and fulfilling to know they are in the community helping others and not just sitting at their home with a "poor me" attitude.

Eric and I sometimes share our stories together at schools, too. We have developed a very powerful presentation. Sometimes Eric, Joyce, and I do the presentation, but other times it's just Eric and me. We travel all over the country together spreading our message. We are trying to make people think and act more responsibly, especially if they are drinking. That is what encouraged me to finally write this book. We want to provoke deep thought and show others the value of making good choices. After reading both of our stories and the consequences following the choices we made, why chance it? I live with regret every day of my life, and Eric does, too. It is what it is and we cannot change our situation, but we can help others if they will let us.

Chapter 11
Eric's Dreams

Hopefully, I played a role in fulfilling one of Eric's dreams. The number eleven is very significant to Eric and he asked if there could be eleven chapters for his story in our book, so I made sure both stories had eleven chapters. Eric's baseball jersey number was eleven. His favorite numbers are eleven (his baseball jersey), fifteen (his football jersey), and seventeen (Tim's baseball jersey). Tim was Eric's friend who died in the crash. This should bring a smile to Eric's face. He is an athlete at heart and has always been superstitious. He believes associating his number with this book will improve our chances of saving lives. That is sincerely both of our dreams.

Eric has many dreams, like walking again, throwing a baseball, getting married (that is a huge dream), going on a TV show to help others through his own story, having a big neon sign that says Eric Krug, and going to a restaurant named Hooters. Eric dreams of his old life, but he is determined to show the world the new Eric in order to help people see the consequences of riding with a drunk driver. Eric also dreams of better adaptive speaking equipment. He has an iPad and it works great, but maybe new technology could improve his quality of life.

I know Eric's biggest dream is for his story to save lives and everyone reading this book could help him fulfill this dream. If anyone reading this book could help fulfill another one of his dreams, contact us, PLEASE! This message is important, and Eric has so much to offer. More people need to meet Eric and see what he is doing with his life.

The Story Behind Eric and Me
Chapter 1
How We Met

While I was in prison, sharing my story under law enforcement custody, Eric and Joyce were sharing their story throughout the state of Georgia. One night at a church, a friend of mine heard them speak. She is my mentor's sister, Elise Lander. She walked up to Joyce and said, "You need to meet my brother, Chad Foster. He is mentoring a guy in prison who is sharing his story with young people about the dangers of drinking and driving." Joyce and Eric found out I was in prison for two counts of vehicular homicide by DUI.

Joyce eventually met Chad, and he convinced her to meet my mom and to come hear me speak. Joyce did not want to meet me, but she was trying her hardest to be open to the idea. Plus, my crash happened on April 11 and Eric's crash happened on April 11. That grabbed our attention and had both of us thinking that perhaps a higher power was trying to bring us together.

I was speaking at a school in Atlanta, Georgia, escorted by deputies. After speaking to the students, Joyce and Eric wanted to talk to me. The deputies were a little hesitant because Joyce and Eric could be there to lash out at me. I was all chained up and not a threat to them, but they had every right to yell and scream at me.

Instead of lashing out at me, Joyce and Eric reached for me and gave me a hug and said, "We forgive you. We are here for you, and your message is powerful. We support you and want you to meet the rest of our family."

Sure enough, I met Eric's dad and sister. They received permission from the warden at my prison to start visiting me. Warden Humphries thought it was a good idea for all involved.

Eventually, we started sharing our stories together in hopes of saving people from making the poor choices of drinking and driving or riding with someone who had been drinking. This was very unique. Something very special was transpiring. An offender and a victim of drinking and driving were joining forces to save lives. This was anything short of a miracle.

Eric and I became friends, and I discovered how truly funny he really is. He jokes with me all the time. Most of the time he is funny, and other times he just thinks he is funny. Either way, Eric's sense of humor is inspiring. He has provided me with evidence for our purpose in life. He makes me believe that God has brought us together for a greater cause.

Chapter 2
Eric Introduces Me to His Sister

While getting to know Eric and his family, I found out how much they had been through. Eric's big dream was to walk his sister, Jennifer, down the aisle, and he did in 2000. In 2003, Jennifer lost her husband. He had heart issues at an early age and died from a massive stroke. They were married for almost three years. It was another devastating blow to the Krug family. This was an event in their life that could not be prevented, unlike my choice to drink and drive or Eric's choice to get into a car driven by someone who had been drinking.

Eric thought it would be a good idea for me to meet his sister. After Eric and Joyce had visited me in prison a few times, Jennifer started coming along as well. She and I began writing to each other, and eventually we wrote to each other every single day for four years. We never missed a day and we became best friends. She knew what pain and guilt felt like so she could understand me. Jennifer was also a believer in my message. We felt as if we were two broken souls brought together to help each other move forward in life.

When I was released from prison, Jennifer and I felt it was time to make a lasting commitment. We were married on October 25, 2009, in Madison, Georgia. Can you guess who my best man was? You got it: Eric.

He even nudged me during the ceremony to tell me, "I hooked you up, so now you gotta hook me up."

A dream of mine is to hook him up with a date someday.

Jennifer informed me she might not be able to have children, which was fine with me. I wanted children, but if she could not, then I was not going to be disappointed. I was blessed to have a woman like Jennifer in my life. Then, another miracle happened in our life. Six months after marriage, we found out we were pregnant with our daughter Madison Rae Sandy, and fourteen months after that, we had Zachary Daniel Sandy. We named him after my dad, Daniel (Dan) Sandy. I sure wish my dad was around to see what I am doing with my life now. He was by my side through some very difficult times in life. He had many disappointments because of my choices, but if he was here now, he would be proud of the direction that my life is taking. My children would have called him Pap Pap. He would have spoiled them rotten, but he would have been the best grandpa ever.

Eric is an awesome uncle. He likes to be called "Unc E". We always say that because he looks and acts like a monkey. Eric has so much fun with the children and he loves them dearly.

Eric will someday live with Jennifer, Madison, Zachary, and me. He lives with his parents now, but at some point in time we will need to take care of Eric. He will always need someone else to care for him because of his lifelong injuries. I look forward to having Eric in our house.

Chapter 3
Our Lives Together

I want to end this book on a positive but serious note. I know there are questions to be answered and essays to be written, but before doing so, I want everyone to know a little more about Eric and me. We crossed each other's paths for a reason. We are here to inspire, educate, and help others with life choices.

I am so thankful for my wife and children, my mom and sister, Eric, Joyce, Jack, John, and their family. We all play a role in each other's lives. I get frustrated at times because I cannot drive my son or daughter around or drive to take my wife on a date, but at least I have my family, and they are here to help me. The choice I made at twenty-two years old is affecting my life now at thirty-five, and will continue to do so for the rest of my life.

My children only know the new Eric, but as they grow we will explain to them what happened. At that time, I will have to tell them what I did. They will probably know this at an early age because if I am allowed to drive in a few years, I will have an ignition interlock system installed in my car. This device will be installed to detect alcohol. I will blow into that machine to start the car and will have to periodically pull over to blow again to keep it running. I do not like the fact that my children and their friends will witness my blowing into the device. There will be a lot of explanations and a lot of reminders of the many consequences related to my decision to drink and drive.

I get extremely frustrated or disappointed at times, but then thoughts of Eric creep into my mind and remind me just how bad it can really be. Eric cannot drive and may never get to experience having his own family. The point is, our lives will always be complicated and overshadowed by our poor choices involving alcohol. We ask that you learn the importance of being responsible and making the right choices to help create more opportunities in your life and allow you to live life without regrets. The victims' family will probably never forgive me for my choice. I will never be able to understand how they feel or the pain I inflicted on their lives. I can only pray for them and hope they will see the good in what I am trying to do with my life. But no matter what I do or say, it will never change what I did. I am trying to move forward so I can help more people. Eric is also moving forward to help others. Moving forward is not an easy task. As much as I have to offer as advice, I still have to listen to others (counselors, authority figures, mentors, and even teens) to keep moving forward and stay focused on my goals.

Learn the value of being responsible through our stories and actually care for the safety of your friends. Please do not be ignorant or selfish and think you are so cool that nothing will ever happen to you, or believe some absurd notion that you drive better when you are drunk. That is so lame. I have heard comments like that by many teens. If you get hurt, injure someone, or even kill someone for thinking like that, you will be saturated in guilt and regret. Become a leader and help others make positive choices in life. Please do not let your friends drink and drive.

"So don't drink and drive . . . or get in a car with a buzzed or drunk driver. You could end up injured just like me"

Eric J. Krug